Broken Things Sing Too

Broken Things Sing Too

Hope the Lionheart

RESOURCE *Publications* • Eugene, Oregon

BROKEN THINGS SING TOO

Copyright © 2026 Hope the Lionheart. All rights reserved. Except for brief quotations in critical publications or reviews, no part of this book may be reproduced in any manner without prior written permission from the publisher. Write: Permissions, Wipf and Stock Publishers, 199 W. 8th Ave., Suite 3, Eugene, OR 97401.

Resource Publications
An Imprint of Wipf and Stock Publishers
199 W. 8th Ave., Suite 3
Eugene, OR 97401

www.wipfandstock.com

PAPERBACK ISBN: 979-8-3852-6640-1
HARDCOVER ISBN: 979-8-3852-6641-8
EBOOK ISBN: 979-8-3852-6642-5
VERSION NUMBER 02/04/26

"This honest woman's memoir recounts a powerful spiritual and personal journey evocative of simultaneously tender love and excruciatingly painful love through the vicissitudes of life and relationships. The inspiring poetry, music lyrics, and heartfelt beauty expressed in these pages warmly grace the reader with both the light of truth and the boldness of hope—in this Jubilee Year of Hope—in often inhospitable places; yet where the Holy Spirit always precedes us. Thank God for the wisdom and resilience of Hope."

—**THOMAS DOUGHERTY**, Director, Center for Speech and Writing, Mundelein Seminary

"In poetry and prose that is both haunting and lyrical, Hope the Lionheart tells a story that wanders through a life of brokenness and healing. Her storytelling is stunning and honest and beautiful. At its heart, it teaches about prayer and the quiet conversation that the Holy One has with each of us, offering mercy and hope no matter where we go in life."

—**CHRISTINA R. ZAKER**, Director of Field Education, Catholic Theological Union

"Nadiya invites the reader into a powerful soul journey marked by suffering, pain, and grief while witnessing to the grace and resiliency of the human spirit. Her vulnerable, creative, and lyrical journey offers the reader new life arising from the ashes of trauma and brokenness."

—**KEVIN P. MCCLONE**, Licensed Clinical Psychologist

"*Broken Things Sing Too* is a compelling novel born out of immense personal and communal suffering, and written by an extraordinary woman of uncommon intellect, courage, and determination whose chosen name is none other than Hope. It is also a song whose rhapsodic and deeply spiritual lyrics invite each reader to listen closely to, and strive to make sense of, their own heart's melody of resilience in the face of life's cruelty and promise."
—Scott C. Alexander, Professor of Islamic Studies and Christian-Muslim Relations, Catholic Theological Union

For the ones who stayed.
And for the ones who couldn't.
For the ones who held my hand when I was silent.
And the ones who never asked me to be someone else.
For the women who prayed me through.
The men who taught me hard truths.
The children who trusted me when I barely trusted myself.
For my homeland—aching and beautiful—and those who still live within its trembling borders.
For the ones who believe in healing, even when the scar is still fresh.
For the ones who lost faith.
And those who rediscovered it.
And above all—For the One who never left, even when I did.
This story is for you.
This song is for all of us.
Because broken things sing too.

This story, though fictional, is inspired by true events.
Names and circumstances have been changed.
The emotions are real.

Contents

Author's Note | ix
Acknowledgments | x

1   Pain | 1
2   Music in My Heart | 3
3   Life Keeps Running | 5
4   Childhood | 7
5   Searching for Meaning | 10
6   The Year the Light Went Out | 13
7   Fast-Growing: Immigration | 17
8   Return | 21
9   Death | 24
10   Vocation | 28
11   Mission | 31
12   Three Years of Hell | 35
13   Do I Have Faith? | 42
14   New Horizons | 45
15   A Friend, a Room, a Question | 48
16   The Darkness of War | 51
17   Men of My Life | 54
18   The Women Who Carried Me | 61
19   Letting Go: The Lioness | 66
20   After | 69
21   When You Don't Belong Anywhere | 72

Contents

22 Invisible Work | 75
23 Why I Still Believe | 77
24 The Church That Hurt Me | 80
25 Grief Comes in Seasons | 83
26 God of the In-Between | 86
27 What I've Learned About Healing | 89
28 Home Isn't a Place | 92
29 Things I Didn't Say | 95
30 What Hope Knows Now | 98

Epilogue: A Letter From Hope | 101

Author's Note

Though this book is written as fiction, every chapter breathes with emotional truth.

The names have changed. The timelines have blurred. But the ache is real. The hope is real. And the journey—in all its mess and wonder—is sacred.

If you recognize parts of yourself in these pages, I pray you feel less alone.

I didn't write this story to be impressive. I wrote it to be honest.

We are all learning how to live with the beauty and brokenness we carry. We are all learning how to sing again—in new languages, in strange places, with trembling voices.

This is my song.

Thank you for listening.

With gratitude,
Hope

Acknowledgments

This book would not exist without those who held space for the story long before it had words.

To the people who walked beside me in silence, in community, in war, in rebuilding—thank you. You taught me that grace often wears a human face.

To the mentors who challenged me, believed in me, and asked the questions I wasn't ready to answer—you made me brave.

To the children, refugees, and forgotten ones I encountered around the world—your resilience shaped my faith more than any theology course.

To my family and friends—especially those who stayed when it was hard—your quiet strength echoes through every chapter.

To the places that held me: the convent, the mission field, the parish, the borrowed rooms, and the chapel floor. Each was holy ground.

To the readers—especially those carrying their own untold stories—may this book remind you: your voice matters, your pain is real, and your healing is sacred.

And finally, to the God who found me in all the wrong places, and loved me still—

Thank you.

1

Pain

Inspired by the Pain That Became the Ink of This Story

The radiator clattered like old bones in the walls. Hope sat curled in her grandmother's chair, knees drawn to her chest, the edges of a wool blanket tucked beneath her chin. The room was dim, lit only by the yellow breath of the hallway light and the pale glow of the city beyond the window. Somewhere out there, life was rushing forward. But in here, time had stopped. Again.

The journal lay open in her lap. The pen she held hovered, but her hand refused to move. Her thoughts were too thick to pour out, too tangled to name.

The pain didn't scream. It didn't even raise its voice. It just returned, patient and certain, like a tide that never forgot the shore.

Hope exhaled shakily. "Why does every man look at me like I belong to him?" she whispered. "Why do they only stay when I let myself disappear?"

Silence answered, as always.

She wiped the back of her hand across her cheek. She hadn't even realized she'd been crying. Again.

Is it me?

Do I make myself invisible, just to be wanted?
Do I even know what love is anymore, or have I just grown good at pretending I do?

She bit the inside of her cheek until the sharpness grounded her. *I'm not a victim,* she reminded herself. *I survived. I always survive.*

Strong. Smart. Resilient. Beautiful. The words rang like hollow medals pinned to a bruised chest.

And yet . . .

The ache returned every time the world grew quiet. Like a phantom limb. Like a black hole, always hungry, always just below the surface.

She whispered her lifeline out loud: "I am good. I am loving. I am enough. This pain will pass."

She said it because she needed to believe it. Because if she didn't say it, the darkness might take root again.

She rocked slightly in the chair, like a child seeking comfort, and let the silence settle around her like a second skin.

Somewhere inside her, beneath the rubble of unanswered questions and broken promises, something small stirred. A whisper of melody. Not yet a song. Just a hint. A vibration.

She wasn't ready to write yet.

But the music had begun.

Echo—Inspired by Pain

Let the silence say what words could not,
The ache that settled deep and hot.
You held your breath to keep from crying,
But even breath begins with dying.
What broke you wasn't just the fall—
It was no one hearing you at all.
Still, somewhere under ash and skin,
A trembling whisper says: begin.

2

Music in My Heart

Inspired by Believing

There are moments when a song cracks open a memory you didn't know was still alive.

Hope sat on the windowsill, her knees tucked under her chin, watching traffic lights bleed into the fog. The city exhaled in colors. She pressed her forehead to the glass and let the hum of music inside her chest speak what she couldn't.

It was a strange thing—still believing.

Still believing that love had meant something. That through all the ache and leaving, there had once been a connection so fierce and bright, it must have come from heaven.

She didn't have the words to describe it anymore. But somewhere inside her, there was a note—soft and persistent—that refused to go silent.

"I still have faith in you," the whisper inside her said.

"Even if I don't know who you are anymore."

She laughed. Quietly. Bitterly. Tenderly.

Then she wrote:

I was so young,
too young to know

*that trying to be everything
often leaves you nothing.
And yet . . . I tried.
I painted walls with secret tears,
filled rooms with dreams,
loved when I had no idea what love meant.
I tried.*

She let the pen fall. The page trembled slightly as the air shifted.

Home. Heart. Faith. All the things that once meant something. Now scattered like songs unfinished.

And still, somewhere under the sorrow—was the music.

Hope closed her eyes.

The song wasn't gone.

It was just beginning again.

3

Life Keeps Running

Inspired by the Agony That Taught Me How to Listen

Life doesn't wait.

Hope once believed that time would pause when the heart broke—that the world might hush itself, if only for a breath, to honor the grief quietly echoing inside her.

But no.

Garbage trucks still roared down the street. The kettle still boiled. Strangers still laughed on balconies. Life kept running like it owed her nothing. Because it didn't.

Hope woke each morning to a strange silence—a fragile second before memory returned.

That moment, that sacred hush before pain remembered itself: she called it "Holy Innocence." A breath before the weight of being.

Sometimes, she lived whole weeks without stumbling. She answered emails. She laughed in the right places. She remembered to water the plant. Life was, at least, functional.

Then—the trigger.

A voice. A smell. A shadow falling just the wrong way across a doorway. And there it was again—the black hole. That old hunger.

The ache that curled beneath her ribs and whispered, "You're not safe. You never were."

"Again?" she would whisper. "You again?"

She never welcomed it. Never could. But there it was, uninvited. And she, trying so hard to pretend she was fine, was not.

Echo—Inspired by the Black Hole

I was too young
to carry that kind of silence.
But I did.
With grace, they said.
With obedience, they meant.
No one saw the girl under the rules.
The ache behind the answers.
The dream that bent itself into shape
until it forgot what it was for.
I didn't choose the storm.
But I learned how to stand in it.
And when I finally spoke,
my voice cracked
the way truth does
when it's been caged too long.

4

Childhood

Part I—The Beginning

Hope was born in winter.

December 28. A quiet, gray kind of day. The kind where even the sky looks tired.

Her father left before she had a name.

He wasn't gone in a dramatic, storybook kind of way. He simply... drifted. First in presence, then in spirit, then entirely. By the time Hope turned one month old, he had vanished from the frame of their lives, like a smudged fingerprint wiped from glass.

Sometimes she wondered if she was born as a tether—her mother's last attempt to make him stay. That thought curled around her early memories like frost on a window. Her mother denied it. "You were named after a song," she'd said, laughing as if that explained everything. "You were my hope. *Nadezhda.*"

But children know. They always know.

From the beginning, Hope felt the need to earn her place. To be beautiful enough. Quiet enough. Smart enough. Anything that might've made him stay.

He never did.

Part II—The Girl Who Trained Instead of Played

Hope learned early that love was scheduled, managed, and measured.

Her mother—fierce, wounded, proud—worked long hours as a mining engineer. It was a job she despised, but it paid for bread and winter coats. The rest was delegated to grandparents, day cares, and disciplines.

At five, Hope was enrolled in rhythmic gymnastics.

Every day after school: stretch, bend, leap, sweat. Her body learned to perform before her mind understood why. Somewhere between the chalky smell of the gym and the ache of split ligaments, she stopped asking for toys. There wasn't time for toys. There was only music and motion and trying to matter.

Hope watched the others twirl—graceful, confident—and wished to *want* it like they did. She didn't. But she *stayed*. Because staying was survival. Because maybe, if she could be extraordinary, someone would notice. Someone would stay.

The coach said she had potential. Maybe even for the Olympics. Hope nodded and trained harder.

Then came the accident—a fall mid-leap that nearly fractured her spine.

The pain became a teacher too.

Part III—Star Student, Ghost Girl

At school, she became "the girl who could do anything."

Top of her class. Fluent in formulas and metaphors. She wrote essays that made teachers pause. She memorized entire chapters from a single reading. It was easy—as long as no one looked too closely.

Girls envied her. Boys adored her. Adults admired her.

Hope felt invisible.

She carried her grandmother's love like a quilt around her shoulders—stitched together from warm meals, soft lullabies, and

Sunday trips for sweets. That love kept her anchored, even when the school corridors felt like minefields.

Once, her teacher called her "too much." Too bright. Too quick. Too outspoken. It wasn't meant as a compliment. It rarely was.

But it didn't stop her. Not then.

She kissed a boy on the cheek in sixth grade and felt her heart stutter. She still remembers the crayons he gave her—the kind with pink and purple in the box. Rare. Treasured.

They called her names behind her back. Prostitute. Tease. Too many boys liked her.

She learned early that to be noticed was dangerous—and being ignored wasn't any safer.

Echo — Inspired by the Quiet Before Everything Falls Apart

Before I had language for grief,
I learned to nod,
to sit still,
to disappear in the right direction.
They called me good.
I mistook that for loved.
The first breaking was not loud.
It was a slow forgetting—
of how to speak,
of how to want,
of how to take up space
without apology.

5

Searching for Meaning

Inspired by Fragments of Loss and Quiet Revelations

There are moments that split a life in two. Before. And after.

For Hope, it was a conversation with her older brother on a heavy winter night when the pipes clanked and the radiators coughed. They sat cross-legged on the floor, sipping tea. Sharing stories like secrets, like offerings.

"I've found the truth," he said. "The real truth."

He told her about a group—they called themselves the Brotherhood of Light. They wore white robes. They chanted mantras. They believed the world would end on a date circled in red: November 24, 1993. They spoke of a messiah born again in a woman's body. Of the final hour. Of cleansing.

Hope was barely twelve.

She didn't understand most of what he said. But something in the urgency of his voice lit a match inside her chest.

What if this life wasn't all there was?

What if—somewhere—there was more?

Searching for Meaning

She started asking questions no one around her could answer. Her schoolbooks weren't enough. Her teachers didn't care. And her church, well . . . her church hadn't really existed yet.

Her brother left home. Walked away from everything—their mother, their grandmother, even the cat—to follow the Brotherhood's prophecies. He fasted. He wandered. He believed.

Her mother broke in slow motion. Hope saw it happen. The silence. The pleading. The calling of strangers who might help.

And then—oddly, beautifully—they started talking.

Hope and her mother had never been close. But now, with her brother gone, they sat side by side on the edge of the couch and spoke of stars and karma, of past lives and the quiet ache that hummed in every human soul.

They joined a group that read Eastern philosophers and meditated by candlelight. People there said that children still saw clearly—their chakras unblocked, their spirits unspoiled.

Hope felt seen.

She was twelve. And for a while, she felt like she belonged.

But something inside her remained restless.

She watched grown men and women speak of peace but fight for power. She watched spiritual leaders fall into the same traps of pride and fear she'd seen in schoolteachers and politicians. She watched love dissolve when ego entered the room.

And she wondered—if we can't save ourselves, who will?

One night, beneath a smoky incense haze, she whispered a quiet question toward the ceiling: *What if none of us can do this alone?*

She didn't get an answer. But she stopped going back.

A half year later, her brother returned.

Gaunt. Hollow-eyed. Starved of both food and truth.

The end of the world hadn't come. The Brotherhood had been arrested. Their messiah? A woman who'd overdosed during an abortion—and later claimed to be the new incarnation of Jesus and Mary. Their followers scattered like ash.

Hope helped nurse him back. Fed him soup in small spoonfuls. Read to him when the silence got too loud. And while her brother drifted between shame and confusion, she turned her gaze somewhere else.

She wasn't sure where she was going.

But she knew what she was leaving behind.

One night, a boy named Andrew—her brother's old friend—invited her to a birthday gathering. He had tried everything, he said: crystals, gurus, temples, silence.

Now he was Catholic.

Hope raised an eyebrow. "You mean incense and Latin and guilt?"

He laughed. "No. Guitars, Bibles, real people."

She didn't believe him. But she went.

And what she found wasn't fire and brimstone. It wasn't chanting or judgment. It was... peace.

Uncomplicated, steady peace.

And for the first time in her life, Hope felt the door inside her heart creak open, just enough for light to slip through.

Echo—Inspired by the Illusion of Arrival

For a while,
the ache quieted.
The candles flickered just right.
The rhythm steadied my breath.
The rules wrapped around me
like soft wool in winter.
I called it home.
I called it peace.
Maybe it was.
Or maybe it was rest
before the storm remembered
where to find me.

6

The Year the Light Went Out

Inspired by Broken Trust and Quiet Resilience

They called her Angel.

It was a nickname from the parish youth group—something lighthearted, affectionate. Hope smiled when she heard it. It made her feel chosen, set apart.

She was sixteen. New to the Church, fresh from a spiritual hunger that had burned through her childhood and left her seeking shelter. She found it under vaulted ceilings, in echoing songs, and in the warm, surprising welcome of a young priest named Father Jonas.

He called her his "youth angel." She glowed in his attention. He was kind, a little disorganized, and had a way of making teenagers feel like the Church belonged to them.

Then one Sunday in late autumn, he was reassigned.

Just like that—gone.

A new priest arrived. Older, sterner. Father Darius.

Hope tried to connect. She offered to help with parish events, sat in front rows, laughed at his half-dry jokes. But he already had a favorite—Luda—and Hope knew how invisible it felt to be second.

Still, she prayed. Every day. That she would be free of jealousy, of need, of the ache to be seen. One evening during the Divine Mercy chaplet, she felt something lift. A grace she didn't expect.

She was free.

And she was alone.

Then came the third priest.

Young. Shy. New. They said he was too gentle for the role, unsure of his footing. So when he noticed Hope—bright, willing, full of ideas—he clung to her presence like a guide rope in fog.

He smiled more when she was around. Asked for her help more than anyone else. Told her she was different.

Hope wanted to believe he saw her soul.

What she didn't realize was that he saw her shadow.

The night it happened was quiet.

She thought it would be a youth gathering—laughter, prayers, music. But no one else arrived. Just the priest. Just her.

She told herself it was fine. That maybe plans had changed. That maybe this was still safe.

There was wine. There were compliments about her hair, her shoulders. A locked door. A missing key. A draft through a hallway.

Then . . . a shadow at the bathroom door. A shape that shouldn't have been there. A breath held too long. A scream swallowed.

She didn't know what had happened—not entirely—only that something was broken. Something invisible. Something sacred.

She didn't finish her tea. She didn't sleep that night.

And the next day, she tried to confess it.

The priest she turned to told her it was all her fault.

That she had tempted a holy priest. That her silence would buy her forgiveness.

Hope left the confessional with shaking hands and a wound no one could see.

The Year the Light Went Out

For months, she walked like a girl who was half ghost. The world continued, but she was somewhere between breath and disappearance. And when the new priest—the one who had confronted her at confession—accused her of being possessed, she almost believed him.

Exorcisms followed. Prayers turned into punishments. Naked hugs and forced kisses became rituals. Blessings crossed lines.

She began to believe that her body was a danger. That love would always disguise itself as harm.

That God had looked away.

Years later, she would write letters. Not to reclaim justice—just to make the silence stop echoing.

One priest apologized. The other didn't.

And the devil? He went quiet when she finally heard different words—spoken not by men, but in prayer, deep and true:

You are my beloved daughter. And what they did was never mine.

That night, she wept into her pillow until the sky turned violet.

She didn't feel holy. Or healed.

But she did feel seen.

And that was something.

Echo—Inspired by the Year the Light Went Out

It didn't feel like violence.
Not at first.
It felt like silence
where there should have been safety.
Like hands that pretended to bless
but only erased.
I left my body to survive.
Watched her fold in on herself,
watched her learn to vanish
to make it stop.

Broken Things Sing Too

They called it discipline.
I called it God.
Until I couldn't.
Something holy was stolen.
Something tender was shattered.
And even now,
when I light the candle,
sometimes it flickers
like it remembers.

7

Fast-Growing

Immigration

Inspired by Hunger, Survival, and the Cost of Growing Up Too Fast

August 1. The year Hope turned eighteen.

She boarded a train with a borrowed coat and a backpack that smelled like home—a home that had stopped offering warmth years ago. Ukraine was breaking. The country held its breath beneath collapsing markets, rising bread prices, and the silent question in every mother's eyes: How will we make it?

Hope had asked herself the same thing. There were no jobs. No money. Just hunger—quiet, constant, humiliating. She had been living on church meals and borrowed kindness for months.

So when a friend called with a chance—a family in Poland looking for a live-in babysitter—she said yes before she could be afraid.

The Polish train felt too clean.

She clutched the seat's armrest like it might disappear. Her stomach ached—partly nerves, partly hunger, partly grief.

When she arrived in the Warsaw suburb, she was led into a dining room that looked like something from a movie: bread, cheese, fruit, coffee, ham—all on one table. She nearly wept.

Her new employers were strangers wearing Catholic masks. The father was loud, charming, and too familiar. His wife smiled from a distance. The child was spoiled, the house too quiet in the wrong ways.

Hope began her routine: wake early, cook, clean, babysit, smile. Her hours blurred. The child screamed. The husband stared. The mother ignored.

Every Sunday, they went to Mass. Perfumed. Polished. Performing.

Hope wondered how God felt about hypocrisy dressed in church clothes.

One evening, as the father passed too close, Hope's breath caught in her throat.

She locked her bedroom door that night. And the night after. And every night after.

She wasn't afraid of the dark—only of what moved within it.

She worked sixteen hours a day. The promised wage—800 zloty—became 400 after a quiet conversation. Hope couldn't argue. She was too tired to fight.

The only light came from outside the house.

She met a boy on the train once—a stranger with kind eyes who offered to show her the city. He brought a friend. They shared jokes and pastries, never pushed, never touched without permission. They spent Sundays together, walking through old Warsaw like children who'd just learned how to laugh.

Hope clung to that.

And then she met Marek.

Marek worked at the advertising agency where Hope helped with layout. He was older—almost twice her age—but he noticed her. Not like the others. Or maybe *exactly* like the others, but more gently.

Fast-Growing

He said she was beautiful. That she had a mind like ink and fire.

She was cold and lonely and barely legal. And flattery had become a kind of warmth she couldn't find anywhere else.

By September, she had moved in with him and his girlfriend. Yes. Both of them.

She slept on a mattress in the corner of their room, next to their German Shepherd. At night, the couple made love behind a paper-thin curtain. Hope closed her eyes and pressed her palms to her ears.

By day, Marek taught her design. Whispered that she was unlike anyone he had known.

By night, he made promises he never kept.

And Hope—still reeling from lost innocence and displacement—let him make her forget.

When the girlfriend found out, it was 3 a.m.

Hope stood in the street holding her backpack while Marek said nothing behind the slammed door. Another man—her boss, this time—picked her up in his car. His girlfriend was in the passenger seat.

Hope didn't love him. But he offered her meals. Shelter. Silence. That was enough.

For a while.

She found a cheap room in the old city, borrowed money to pay rent, and slept on the floor until her first paycheck came. Every choice felt like survival, not betrayal. Every compromise a calculation.

She kept working. Kept trying. Kept waking up.

Because beneath the hunger, the fear, the exhaustion—she still believed there had to be something better.

Something more than being used. Something more than just enduring.

Something holy.

Echo—Inspired by Immigration, Resilience, and the Speed of Becoming

I grew faster than I should have.
Because I had to.
New streets,
new tongue,
new rules no one explained.
There wasn't time to mourn
what I left behind.
Only time to translate,
to smile,
to survive.
I carried a country in my chest
and learned how to hide it.
Growing up wasn't gradual.
It was demanded.
And still,
a part of me stayed small
and waited
to be missed.

8

Return

Inspired by St. Augustine's Longing and the Scent of Something Holy

Hope didn't come back to church because of theology. She came back because of *longing*.

It wasn't dramatic. There were no visions. Just the ache—deep and low—that hummed beneath everything she did. A homesickness of the soul.

She had walked far from where she started. Lovers who never knew her name. Rooms with locked doors. Workplaces where men saw her as decoration, not design.

Some nights she sat on her rented floor, coat still on, holding a cold cup of tea and whispering, "Is anyone coming for me?"

No one came.

But something stirred.

She wandered into a church one afternoon—old, carved, and shadowy—tucked between rows of flower stalls and bookshops in downtown Warsaw. A Dominican parish. The door creaked. The air inside was thick with incense and dust.

She wasn't sure why she stayed.

A flyer pinned near the confessional caught her eye:
Charismatic Prayer Group—Tuesdays at 7
Come as you are.
She nearly laughed at the irony. *If only you knew who I am.*
But the ache was louder than her pride.
So she went.

The group wasn't what she expected.

No hysteria. No forced joy. Just people—ordinary, broken, hungry—singing softly, praying out loud in voices that trembled like hers.

During Lent, they studied the story of the prodigal son. Hope sat in the back, scribbling lines of Scripture in her notebook like they might save her.

One verse caught her like a thread through the ribs:

"While he was still a long way off, his father saw him and was filled with compassion."

She closed her eyes.

What if God hadn't moved?

What if He had been standing at the edge of the road the entire time?

She made an appointment for confession.

This time, there was no condemnation. No silence. Just a gentle voice on the other side of the screen saying, "You are seen. You are loved. Begin again."

She wept until her coat sleeves were soaked through.

Soon after, during a group retreat, she met Father Elijah.

He was kind, older, quiet. He didn't flinch at her questions. He didn't rush her prayers. When she told him pieces of her story—not the whole thing, but enough—he listened.

"You're still here," he said. "That's already grace."

Hope didn't know if she believed him.

But she wanted to.

Return

The road back wasn't linear.

She still felt panic in the pews sometimes. Still flinched at kindness. Still doubted that God could want what was left of her.

But she kept showing up.

One night, kneeling in the silence after Mass, she whispered, "If you don't mind broken things . . . you can have what's left of me."

And in the quiet, she swore she felt it—not thunder. Not fire.

Just the warmth of a father running toward his daughter.

Echo—Inspired by Returning to God from the Far Places

I didn't know how to come back.
I only knew how to ache.
I thought He'd be angry.
Or distant.
Or worse—silent.
But He was there.
Not waiting like a judge,
but watching like a Father
who never stopped calling me home.
I was still bleeding.
Still half-gone.
Still unsure if I was worth the reaching.
And yet,
He ran.

9

Death

Inspired by Breathless Nights and Burning Clarity

Death didn't come like she expected.

It didn't come with sirens or flashing lights. It didn't ride in like a villain cloaked in shadow.

It came in stillness—a quiet room, a swelling throat, and the steady realization that no one was coming.

It was spring. Hope had caught something again—the kind of illness that clung to her chest and refused to let go. Her lungs burned. Her throat tightened. She'd been coughing for days, too stubborn to rest, too afraid to ask for help.

She had argued with Father Elijah that week. Over something small, probably. But the ache of being misunderstood lingered. She hadn't heard from him since.

That night, alone in her Warsaw apartment, her breath started to slip.

First, slowly. Then all at once.

She tried sitting up. Sipping water. Praying.

Nothing worked.

Death

Her phone buzzed on the nightstand. With shaking fingers, she typed out a message to him.

"I can't breathe."

Sent.

Sent again.

Twelve times.

She never knew if he got it. Or if he thought she was being dramatic. After all, she'd always been too sensitive, too intense, too much.

But this time, it wasn't panic. It wasn't emotion.

It was her body—quietly folding in on itself.

And then...

The room changed.

Suddenly, she wasn't on her mattress. She was standing barefoot on a wide green meadow. The air was too still. The colors too sharp. It didn't feel like a dream.

Before her stood a mound of scorched earth, as if a house had burned down and only the chimney stones remained. The smell of smoke lingered, though the fire was long gone.

An angel stood nearby. Or something like an angel. Tall. Pale. Sad-eyed.

He nodded toward the ruins.

"These are your deeds," he said. "All that you've done."

She looked closer.

Each blackened stone shimmered with memory. Failures. Betrayals. Moments she hadn't forgiven herself for.

"There's no point in facing Him," the angel continued. "You'll be judged. You know what you've done. Just walk away now—spare yourself the shame."

Hope stared at the scorched pile.

It felt true.

Too true.

She turned to leave.

Then paused.

Something inside her stirred.

A small defiant voice—the one that always came when she was just about to disappear.

Wait.

Where are the others?

Where were the nights she had brought soup to her brother after the cult had shattered him?

The hours she'd stayed on the phone with broken girls, holding their hearts in her trembling hands?

The mornings she rose early to pray, not because she had to, but because she still wanted to believe?

She turned back to the angel.

"I don't see the love."

The angel didn't speak.

Hope stepped forward.

"I know what I've done. But I know what I've given too."

And with that, she walked toward the mountain path—the one that led toward the light.

Her body lay still on the mattress. But her soul remembered that moment forever. Moment of love. Infinite love.

She didn't die.

But something inside her did.

The lie that she was unworthy. That she was only her worst day. That her value was measured in pain.

She let that version of herself go.

And when the breath finally returned, slow and burning, she whispered, "He wants me to live. I have a mission."

Echo—Inspired by Clinical Death and What Remains

I let go.
Not with fear—
but with a strange, slow mercy.
The noise disappeared.

Death

So did the reasons,
the striving,
the proving.
There was only love.
Not remembered—
known.
Like light you don't look at,
only feel.
Nothing else followed me there.
Not titles,
not fear,
not even regret.
Only love.
And it was enough.
More than enough.

10

Vocation

Inspired by Quiet Callings and Inconvenient Grace

Hope didn't believe in signs.

At least, not the obvious kind. Not burning bushes or angelic visitations or thunderclaps behind altars. No, the voice that called her came like most truths do: soft, persistent, and entirely inconvenient.

After her near-death night, she began to walk differently. Not with certainty—but with weight. Like someone entrusted with something delicate, though she didn't know what it was yet.

She kept showing up at church. The pews stopped feeling hostile. The prayers stopped sounding foreign. The hunger that once drove her into dark corners now pulled her toward something quieter. Simpler. Sacred.

It wasn't dramatic.

Just . . . steady.

One day, during Mass, she stayed after the final blessing. The others left. Coats rustled. Doors closed.

Hope remained in her place, eyes unfocused, hands still.

Vocation

And then it came—not in words, not even in feeling, but in *knowing*.

Give your life to me.

She didn't know if it came from God or her own aching hope. But it was clear.

She told no one at first.

It felt absurd. Her? A religious sister? After everything?

She could already hear the laughter. See the raised eyebrows. The girl who was used and discarded, who had slept on floors and in strangers' beds, who'd lost her innocence in the name of trust—now wants to become holy?

It felt like a joke.

Except it didn't feel like one to God.

Eventually, she whispered the thought to Father Elijah.

He didn't laugh.

He didn't flinch.

He only asked, "What makes you think He hasn't been calling you all along?"

Hope looked down at her hands—scarred in places no one could see—and said quietly,

"Because I'm not good enough."

Elijah smiled.

"Then you're exactly who He calls."

She began visiting religious communities. Not all were kind. Some saw only her age. Some saw only her past.

But one place felt different. A small missionary order, tucked behind a church with peeling paint and a courtyard that smelled like rosemary and coal. The sisters laughed with their whole bodies. They made bread and buried the dead and taught children how to pray with crayons.

Hope watched them move and thought, This is how I want to be loved. And this is how I want to love.

She filled out the application form with trembling hands.

Name: Hope.

Reason for applying: I think I've been searching for this all my life.

The journey would not be easy.
There were still nights of doubt. Still mornings when she looked in the mirror and asked, Who do you think you're fooling?
But the ache had shifted.
It was no longer a hunger for someone to claim her.
It was a desire to *belong*—to the One who had always been waiting.

Echo—Inspired by the Vow, the Veil, and the Voice That Said Yes

I gave Him everything
because it felt like love.
Because I needed something
pure,
clear,
undivided.
I wore the veil
like a promise I didn't know how to keep
but longed to.
They called it a vow.
To me, it felt like an exhale.
Like finally being wanted
for what I didn't need to earn.
I didn't know yet
that surrender is only the beginning.
But in that moment,
I was His.
And that was enough.

11

Mission

Inspired by a Restless Heart and the Strange Grace of Foreign Soil

Hope didn't become holy when she took her first vows.
    She didn't feel clean, or pure, or entirely ready. But she felt willing. That was enough.
    She had chosen a life that didn't promise comfort. One that asked for everything and offered no guarantees—only the wild possibility that Love could be lived in flesh, in feet, in broken languages, in dusty train stations and crowded orphanages.
    And so, she was sent.

Siberia

Cold was not the worst part.
    The worst part was the silence.
    Hope worked at a children's center where addiction and absence were inherited like family recipes. The kids were too quiet. Their eyes too old. Some flinched when touched.

She taught songs and colors and numbers. She poured soup into trembling hands and swept the floors at night when no one could see her cry.

One boy—Vania—used to sleep under her desk during playtime. He said it was the only place he didn't dream of fire.

Hope learned not to ask too many questions.

She also learned that love, here, was not a feeling. It was a scarf tied gently. A story repeated for the hundredth time. A goodbye that did not come too soon.

Slovakia

She was sent to teach media classes to Roma teenagers.

The other sisters warned her: *They won't listen. They won't care.*

But Hope did not expect obedience. She expected chaos.

Instead, she found artistry. Sass. Raw brilliance hidden beneath bruised reputations.

She taught them how to film their stories—their way. The cameras became confessions. The microphones, freedom.

She never forgot one girl—Luma—who whispered, "Miss Hope, I didn't think we were allowed to matter."

Hope swallowed hard.

"Who told you that?"

Luma just shrugged.

Hope made a silent vow that every lesson from then on would be a rebellion against that lie.

The Philippines

Heat. Laughter. Layers of sorrow under song.

She worked in a center for women who had been sold, traded, discarded.

Some days were full of dance and coconut rice and bracelets made from discarded wire.

MISSION

Other days . . . they were not.

She sat with women who could not say what had happened to them, only show it in the way their hands wouldn't unclench.

She didn't preach. She didn't fix. She just stayed.

That was her offering.

And somewhere between prayer circles and healing workshops, she realized that she was not just the missionary.

She was also the wounded one being healed.

Poland

Final vows. Back in Europe. A chapel with creaky floors and candles that flickered even without wind.

The ceremony was simple. A white dress. A veil. A whispered yes. A controversial dance.

Her name—Sister Hope—was spoken aloud like a second birth.

People smiled. Applauded. Took pictures.

But that night, in her tiny room under the rafters, she cried alone.

Not from regret.

From the strange beauty of it all.

That a girl who had been left, betrayed, starved, and forgotten . . . was now called "bride of Christ."

That she, too, had been chosen—not in spite of her scars, but because of them.

She was still learning how to belong.

But she was no longer searching.

She had found her place in the in-between—the holy space where pain becomes service and survival becomes song.

Echo—Inspired by a Life Poured Out on Foreign Soil

I came to give
but left with pieces I hadn't planned to lose.
The faces stayed.
The hunger.
The barefoot children.
The old woman who called me *daughter*.
I thought I was bringing God with me.
But He was already there—
in the smell of rice,
the cut of winter wind,
the eyes that asked me to see
without fixing.
Mission didn't make me holy.
It made me human.
And I bled quietly into every goodbye
I didn't want to say.

12

Three Years of Hell

Part I—Inspired by the Silence That Follows Betrayal

Not all wounds are made by strangers.

Hope once believed the worst had already happened—that once she wore the veil, the past would stay behind her. That community meant safety. That sisterhood would protect her from the world's noise and harm.

She was wrong.

It began with a change in assignments.

New superiors. New expectations. New community.

From the outside, it looked ordinary. A missionary returning home, ready to serve. But the air in this new house was thick with something unseen. A slow poison.

Hope was too eager at first—too ready to prove herself. She tried to be helpful, obedient, invisible. But her presence seemed to ignite something in others. Jealousy, maybe. Distrust. Or just old pain that needed somewhere to land.

They called her too proud. Too sensitive. Too emotional. Too much.

Again.

Every day became a performance.

She monitored her tone. She trimmed her words. She stepped carefully through conversations as if the floors might give way.

Small humiliations gathered like stones in her pocket.

Her schedule was changed without warning. Her requests denied without reason. Her letters went unanswered. Her silence was expected. Her gifts were treated like threats.

One sister said to her, flatly, "You're not like us."

Hope wanted to ask, *What does that mean?* But she already knew.

She was the one who didn't know how to pretend.

The hardest part wasn't the cruelty. It was the gaslighting.

She was told she was imagining things.

That she needed deeper humility.

That perhaps she was being purified.

She began to doubt her own memory. Her own motives. Her own worth.

There were days she prayed, not to be holy, but to disappear.

Once, she asked her superior if she could take a silent retreat—just a weekend to breathe, to think.

The answer was sharp: "You're not trustworthy. You'll run away."

Hope nodded, smiled, and returned to work.

But something inside her cracked.

At night, she wrote letters she never sent.

To God. To the girl she used to be. To the version of herself that once believed in the Church with childlike awe.

Why didn't You come for me?

Why did You let this happen in Your name?

Am I still Yours?

Silence answered.

But sometimes, in that silence, she could almost hear a heartbeat that wasn't her own.

The turning point came slowly.
One evening, after another sharp correction for something she hadn't done, Hope walked past the chapel.
She didn't go in.
She didn't kneel.
She just whispered, "I don't think I believe in You anymore."
And then, softer: "But I miss You."

Part II—Fire Within Fire

The Accident

And the fire kept coming.
The darkness didn't stop with words.
She remembers the smell first.
Burnt rubber. Dust. Blood and something metallic—like rust and lightning.
One moment she was driving home from a retreat. The next, the world flipped sideways.
The car in the other lane had been going too fast. Hope saw it a second too late—just enough time to say God's name, but not enough to hear an answer.
The crash wasn't loud. It was *final*.
She woke up upside down.
The windshield shattered. The world spinning in slow motion. Her crucifix dangling from the mirror like a question mark.
Someone pulled her out. She doesn't remember who.
She walked away from the wreckage with a bruised shoulder, two cracked ribs, and a silence inside her that lasted for months.
People called it a miracle.
Hope called it unfinished business.
Something in her spirit had left the car before the impact. And for a long time afterward, she felt as if it hadn't come back.

The Man in the Gray Office

It wasn't called the KGB anymore.

But the office smelled the same—bleach, bureaucracy, and fear.

They called her in under the pretense of "verifying a report." No warning. No lawyer. No clear accusation. Just a seat across from a man who didn't blink enough and never used her full name.

He asked about the retreat. About her trips abroad. About the children's center in Siberia.

About the letters she'd sent to a friend in Ukraine. About the priest she'd mentioned once in an email.

Hope kept her hands folded and her eyes steady. "I don't understand what you're asking."

He smiled.

It wasn't a kind smile.

"I think you do," he said. "You've seen things. You've met people."

Then he leaned forward, as if offering a favor.

"You're smart, Sister. Stay quiet. Pray your prayers. And don't dig too deep."

That night, Hope lay awake in her room, wondering what file her name was printed on. What photograph they had clipped into a manila folder.

She wasn't afraid of being watched.

She was afraid of being erased. Then there was the man with the sharp suit and a sharper agenda.

He never introduced himself, not fully. But Hope knew who he was. You didn't grow up in post-Soviet silence without recognizing the scent of surveillance.

He asked questions that weren't really questions.

He knew too much.

He hinted at files. At things better left buried. At people who still watched from behind lace curtains and mirrored glasses.

KGB may have changed names. But fear didn't.

Three years of interrogating. Twice a week for three hours. Hope left those conversations feeling scraped raw—not by violence, but by *invisibility*. Like her life was someone else's game.

My Brother, Again

The call came during Adoration.
    She almost didn't pick up. But something in her bones said: *answer it*.
    Her brother was gone.
    Again.
    This time it wasn't the Brotherhood of Light. It was something newer, more polished. A group that used different language—freedom, healing, ascension—but held the same grip. They had drawn him in with meditations and prophecies and promises of power.
    He had not packed his things. Left no note. Taken. Disappeared. Kidnapped.
    Hope sat on the chapel floor long after the call ended. Everyone expected her to save him.
    It was a wound reopening. A film playing again, with new actors but the same ending.
    She remembered being twelve, hearing him describe his white robe with pride. Remembered the morning the police dragged dozens of "disciples" out of Saint Sophia Cathedral for dancing on the altar, proclaiming the world's end.
    She remembered spoon-feeding him soup after the arrest, after ten days without food or water. His hands shaking. His eyes lost.
    And now—again.
    He had followed someone claiming to be the voice of truth. Again.
    Only this time, there might not be a police report. No rescue. Just silence.
    She had thought those days were behind them—the white-robed cult, the false messiahs, the chanting that hollowed people out.

She couldn't breathe when she heard the news.

It was as if time folded in on itself and she was twelve again, standing in the doorway as her brother packed a bag and walked away from everything they were.

She couldn't find him.

All she could do was remember: the child who used to hold her hand on the way to school, who gave her his last candy on cold days, who once told her, "If anything happens, I'll protect you."

And now he was the one who needed saving.

Those three years held more than pain.

They held fire.

Not the kind that warms or refines, but the kind that *consumes*—that eats through every carefully constructed belief and leaves only ash and the echo of unanswered prayers.

Hope survived it. She survived hell.

But she did not emerge untouched.

Eventually, the community moved her to another assignment. Whether to protect her or punish her, she never knew.

The damage was already done.

Three years. Three years of soul-fracture. Of keeping her hands folded while her insides bled. Of surviving not just the world, but the people who spoke the name of Christ while wounding in His place.

She would never forget it.

She would never return to that house.

But she would, somehow, keep walking.

Because even in hell—Hope still refused to die.

She lit a candle that night.

Not to make a request.

Just to let God know she was still here.

Still watching.

Still waiting.

Three Years of Hell

Echo—Inspired by Trauma, Silence, and the Cost of Being Unseen

They didn't kill me.
They just watched me disappear.
Day by day,
name by name,
I unraveled
under the weight of what no one would say out loud.
I stopped asking for help.
They taught me not to.
I became what they needed—
quiet,
useful,
broken enough
to make their comfort work.
No one fought for me.
So I learned to fight silence with silence.
And when they finally let me go,
I was already gone.

13

Do I Have Faith?

Inspired by Ashes, Silence, and the Flicker That Stays Lit

Hope didn't lose her faith all at once.

It unraveled like thread from an old sweater—slow, quiet, almost imperceptible at first. A skipped prayer here. A missed Mass there. Then entire weeks passed without the taste of a psalm.

She still wore the veil. Still showed up when required. Still bowed at the right moments.

But inside?

Inside, everything was hollow.

She kept trying to believe.

Because it's what good sisters did. Because she had taken vows. Because people were watching.

But sometimes, during liturgy, she would stare at the host and whisper, "Are You really there? Or are we all pretending together?"

No lightning struck.

No voice answered.

And so she did what she had always done when abandoned.

She endured.

Do I Have Faith?

She went through the motions. Helped with meals. Smiled in photos. Led reflections. All while feeling like a fraud.

Hope didn't feel angry anymore. Anger had burned out during those three years of quiet cruelty.

What she felt now was tired. Tired of trying. Tired of faking certainty. Tired of trusting the Church, who gaslit. Tired of waiting for God to intervene and *not* getting an answer.

The question she had never dared to say aloud now rang louder than any hymn:

Do I still believe?

She tried to confess it once.

Not a sin, exactly. More like a disorientation.

The priest—younger than her, nervous—told her she needed more Eucharistic Adoration.

She nodded. Smiled.

And walked out feeling lonelier than before.

But one evening, long after Compline, she passed the chapel and stopped at the door.

The sanctuary lamp glowed red—soft, steady, like the last coal in a dying fire.

She sat in the back pew.

No words. No petitions. No bargain.

Just breath.

And slowly, a realization rose—not like revelation, but like remembering.

Faith wasn't a feeling.

It wasn't certainty.

It wasn't clarity or warmth or theological proofs.

Faith was showing up when you don't want to.

Faith was lighting a candle when the wind is howling.

Faith was returning—even if you're limping, silent, and unsure.

She whispered that night, "I don't know what I believe right now. But I still want You. And maybe that's enough."

She felt nothing in return.
But she stayed.
And that—for the first time in a long while—felt like the beginning of faith again.

Echo—Inspired by the Silence After the Collapse of Meaning

I wasn't sure what I believed.
Only that I missed Him.
The prayers tasted like ash.
The rituals, empty.
And still—
something deeper than thought
kept reaching.
I didn't feel faith.
But I couldn't forget Him.
Even in the dark,
I whispered into the silence,
not because I was certain,
but because I still hoped
He was the kind who listens
when no one else is left.

14

New Horizons

Inspired by Long Flights, Short Prayers, and Unexpected Landscapes

The plane landed with a thud—as if the earth itself was unsure about her arrival.
    Hope had never been to America.
    In truth, she had never *dreamed* of coming. Not because she didn't care—but because it had always seemed like a place from television: too shiny, too loud, too far away to be real.
    But now she was here.
    A convent. A ministry assignment. A suitcase. A map she couldn't read.
    America was too big—in every way.

Everything felt upside-down.
    People smiled at strangers. Clergy wore sneakers. Grocery stores had twenty kinds of toothpaste. The churches were modern and spotless, but somehow . . . *hollow*.
    Hope couldn't name it at first.
    Only that she missed incense. Silence. The kind of Mass that took its time.

Here, everything seemed fast. Casual. Marketed.

She remembered kneeling in a parish where the tabernacle was hidden behind a plant and wondering, *Do they even know He's here?*

She didn't say it aloud. That kind of thought could get you labeled "rigid" or "unpastoral."

But she couldn't help grieving something unnamed.

Her community was kind. Mostly.

But tired. Stretched thin. Caught between ministries and meetings and spreadsheets. They meant well—but didn't always listen.

Hope was asked to help with parish outreach. She said yes, as she always did.

Catechesis, food pantry, Bible study.

But the children didn't understand her accent.

The adults didn't understand her silence.

She gave talks that fell flat. Smiled through meetings where no one asked her story. Her past felt like a secret no one wanted to unlock.

She missed the Philippines. Missed the chaos and clarity of suffering that made every small act of kindness feel holy.

Here, people complained about coffee brands and carpet colors in the parish hall.

One night, at a committee meeting about liturgy font sizes, Hope excused herself and went to the empty chapel.

She sat in the dark and whispered, "Lord, I didn't come here for fonts."

She half-expected God to laugh.

But instead, she felt something quieter.

Like permission.

Despite it all, she kept showing up.

She visited the sick. She hugged the awkward kids. She made pierogi for the nuns who missed their mothers.

One woman, recently widowed, broke down in the parish parking lot. Hope didn't offer answers. She just sat on the curb with her until the sobbing stopped.
    That's when she began to understand:
    In America, the wounds were hidden.
    Dressed in suits. Covered by smiles. Decorated with busy calendars.
    But they were still wounds.
    And maybe her own brokenness could still speak here—even if her language faltered.

She didn't feel at home.
    Not yet.
    But she stayed.
    Because she was no longer chasing belonging.
    She was becoming it.

Echo—Inspired by Arrival and the Ache of Beginning Again

I came with everything I had—
which wasn't much
except for grief,
and a name I still wasn't sure belonged to me.
The sky was wider here.
The silence different.
But the ache followed,
quietly packed between visa papers and half-buried prayers.
I didn't know if this place would hold me.
But I was too tired to run.
Too lonely not to hope.
So I unpacked slowly.
And let the light touch
what I hadn't dared to show
even to myself.

15

A Friend, a Room, a Question

**Inspired by Unexpected Friendships
and the Soft Return of Self**

The question came on a Tuesday.

Not in a confessional or classroom—but over a chipped mug of tea, while folding parish bulletins with a woman named Marla, who had been divorced twice, loved jazz, and prayed like God was her roommate.

"Have you ever told your story?" she asked casually.

Hope blinked.

"What do you mean?"

"I mean the real one."

Hope smiled politely. "Parts of it."

Marla raised an eyebrow. "Parts don't heal people. Wholeness does."

She didn't push. Just handed Hope another bulletin to fold.

"When you're ready," she added, "I'll listen."

Later that night, in her small convent room, Hope found herself staring at a blank notebook.

She hadn't opened it in months.

A Friend, a Room, a Question

She'd come to the US to serve. To prove her worth. Not to dig through memories like broken china. But now, the silence in her chest begged to be translated.

She wrote one sentence: *God finds us where we pretend the least.*

And closed the notebook.

A month later, Marla invited her to a retreat. "Come tell your story," she said.

Hope laughed. "Who would want to hear that?"

Marla only smiled.

"Someone who's bleeding quietly."

The room was plain. Folding chairs. A cross made of driftwood.

Hope stood with her notes clutched like armor. Then, without looking down, she said, "I used to think holiness was for the unbroken. Now I know—it's the ones who bleed *and stay*."

There was silence.

Then a woman in the back began to cry.

Hope didn't stop her.

She only said, "If He can still use me, He can still use you too."

That night, she opened her notebook again and wrote, *I'm not healed. But I'm real. And that's a beginning.*

Echo—Inspired by the Moment the Story Began to Speak

It started with a question—
casual,
kind,
unexpected.
And suddenly,
the silence I had carried like a shield
cracked.
Not all the way.

Broken Things Sing Too

Just enough
for truth to breathe.
There was no plan.
Just a laptop,
a couch,
a heart that had waited too long
to be listened to.
I didn't write to heal.
I wrote because
the story was tired of hiding.

16

The Darkness of War

Inspired by Sirens on the Screen and Prayers with No Language

Hope was making tea when the war began.

The news had been simmering for weeks—border tensions, satellite images, talking heads. But it still felt unreal. Like the kind of fear that lives behind glass.

Until February 24.

She was in the parish kitchen when Marla burst in, phone in hand, face pale.

"It's started."

Hope didn't need to ask what.

She sat down slowly, one hand still holding a spoon.

The rest of the day blurred.

News feeds. Explosions. Cities she knew reduced to smoke. Children hiding underground. Her mother's village—the one with the lilac trees—mentioned in the crawl beneath the footage of tanks.

She called home.

The line rang. Then nothing.

She called again. Then again.

When her mother finally answered, her voice was steady—too steady.

"We're staying," she said. "If we run, where would we go?"

Hope sat on her convent bed and wept. Not loudly. Just the kind of crying that empties the bones.

Suddenly, everything she did in the US felt *useless*.

Catechism classes. Potluck planning. Bulletin proofreading. What did any of it matter when her people were bleeding?

She wanted to fly back. Do something. Hold someone. Hide someone. Shout into the world's apathy until it cracked.

But she couldn't.

So she did what she could.

She organized drives. Collected donations. Translated letters. Spoke on panels. Wrote grant proposals. Baked bread for vigils.

She prayed.

More than ever.

Less than ever.

Because sometimes the prayers were just silence.

And sometimes they were fists.

One night, at a parish Holy Hour, someone lit a candle for Ukraine and mispronounced its name.

Hope almost screamed.

She didn't.

She just walked outside into the snow and let herself break open.

In the months that followed, her life split in two.

In the daylight, she was the calm Sister with the clipboard.

At night, she read reports from Kyiv and Kharkiv, Donetsk, and Mariupol until her vision blurred.

She stopped watching the footage. But the sirens still rang in her dreams.

The Darkness of War

What no one saw was the shift.

    Something cracked—not just in her heart, but in her calling.

    The war had not only shaken her homeland.

    It had shaken her *vows*.

    Because how do you remain obedient when your soul is shouting in another direction?

Echo—Inspired by the War That Changed Everything

I woke up
and my country was bleeding.
No sirens in my room.
But I felt it—
in my chest,
in my knees,
in the way prayer turned into begging.
I watched from safety
and still couldn't breathe.
I called my mother,
my brother,
my God.
None of them could stop the noise.
So I lit a candle,
and tried to keep it from going out
while the world burned.

17

Men of My Life

Some I Loved. Some I Forgave.
Some I'm Still Figuring Out

This chapter doesn't move in time.
    It moves in ache. In memory. In fragments.
    Not all these men were villains. Not all were saints.
    But each left a mark.
    This chapter doesn't follow time.
    It follows heartbeat.
    Memory.
    Grief.
    And the strange men who taught her about herself—sometimes by staying, but more often, by leaving.

Simba

His real name doesn't matter. She called him Simba—not because he roared, but because something inside him refused to stay small. He called her Sister Lioness.

He loved her with an honesty she hadn't known was possible—not the kind that demanded, but the kind that saw. Really saw. Past the habit. Past the scars. Into the woman beneath it all.

He told her she was wild. That she didn't need permission to be whole.

Hope had never thought of herself as brave—not really. But when he looked at her, she believed she could become someone new. Someone unafraid. She could do anything.

His love didn't rescue her.

It released her.

And when they parted, it wasn't because the love ended.

It was because she had finally started writing her own story.

Mr. Paris

He opened the world.

She met him in a time when her voice was still tucked into the folds of obedience—careful, measured, never too loud.

He didn't pull her out of the shell. He *invited* her out—gently. With questions. With wonder. With the kind of curiosity that made her feel like her thoughts mattered, not just her presence.

He taught her to notice beauty. To think big. To sit at the table like she belonged there.

He never crossed a line.

But he stood close to the edge—and so did she.

He didn't give her answers.

He gave her possibility.

And to this day, when she speaks with clarity, when she dares to walk through the open door, she knows a part of that courage came from him.

Mr. Possessive

He could have been a chapter.

But he wanted to be the whole book.

He met her when she was fragile but rebuilding—when her faith was shifting and her feet were barely steady.

He was brilliant. Intense. And deeply afraid of his own softness.

He offered certainty, systems, a plan.

She offered questions, risk, wonder.

He called it fascinating instability.

She called it simply becoming.

What began as admiration became control—soft, subtle, but tightening like a thread. She couldn't breathe.

He loved her, yes.

But he wanted to contain her.

And Hope had already broken out of too many cages to walk into another.

When he finally stepped away, it hurt.

Because love was never the question.

But freedom was always the answer.

Mr. Friendly

He was high-strung, brilliant, perpetually persistent, too organized, and absolutely certain he was meant for something extraordinary.

Hope initially found him irritating. Then oddly fascinating. Then . . . familiar.

He asked her too many questions.

She gave too few answers.

One night, while walking to the train station, he said, "You confuse me. I think I'm either supposed to fall in love with you or become a monk."

Hope laughed. "Then I've done my job."

He chuckled, but looked at her like she held a mirror to something he wasn't ready to see.

They stopped talking months later. No falling out. Just a slow fade.

Hope still wonders sometimes what would've happened if one of them had been braver.

Men of My Life

My Father

The first man. The one who was supposed to stay.

Hope remembers his hands—always moving, holding a cigarette, making plans.

She also remembers the silence when he left.

The phone that didn't ring.

The birthdays that passed like pages skipped in a book.

She told herself she didn't need him.

But every time a man walked away, it was his shadow she saw first.

The Priest

He had a voice like gravel and incense. Hope once believed he knew God personally.

He praised her faith. Said she had a "vocation fire." Gave her theology books and tender glances that confused her.

One day, he confessed his love. Quietly. After confession. In the sacristy.

She froze.

She said nothing.

He left the priesthood a year later.

She told no one for a long time.

Because what do you say when a man you trusted with your soul tells you he wants your body?

Father in Every Way but Name

There was one more.

He was a priest—a complicated, radiant soul who stepped into Hope's life like the father she never had.

He was passionate, theatrical, full of conviction and full of contradictions. He could command a liturgy like it was a symphony. He could make a whole room lean in with a single whispered word of blessing.

But he was also terrified of tears. "Whenever a woman cries near me," he confessed, "I panic." He wanted so badly to fix what couldn't always be fixed.

He held high standards—for himself first. He expected holiness, craved beauty, and searched for God in every aching detail of daily life.

Hope leaving for the convent broke something in him. Her silence in Siberia broke the rest.

He didn't always understand her, but he always loved her—in his flawed, reverent, fiercely human way.

A priest.

A mentor.

A mirror of both tenderness and tension.

And like the others, he left fingerprints on the soul she was becoming.

My Brother

Lost and found and lost again.

Hope loved him with the desperation of a child trying to hold back an avalanche.

He disappeared into cults, into silence, into worlds she couldn't reach.

But when he laughed, he sounded like home.

She never stopped loving him.

She never will.

He was a home. A heart of her heart. A soul of her soul.

The Stranger on the Plane

He saw her veil and asked, "So ... are you like a nun?"

She smiled politely. "Something like that."

He didn't stop talking for two hours.

Told her about his divorce, his regrets, his theories on why people stopped going to church.

She nodded, listened.

Before landing, he said, "You're the only person I've told that stuff to."

Sometimes, Hope wonders if God uses her silence more than her sermons.

The Old Man with the Cane

He came to daily Mass. Sat in the last pew. Never spoke.

One day, he handed her a folded note.

"You remind me of my daughter. She died last year. Thank you for standing where she can't."

She cried in her car for twenty minutes.

The Boy Who Said Sorry

He was thirteen.

At a retreat. Smart mouth. Loud jokes.

He interrupted her testimony to say, "You talk like pain made you better. That's messed up."

Later, he came up, eyes wide.

"I'm sorry. I didn't mean it like that. It's just . . . I don't want to hurt like that."

She knelt beside him. Said, "Neither did I."

They cried together.

She never saw him again.

But she carries that moment like a relic.

Christ

The only Man who never flinched.

When she raged, He stayed.

When she ran, He waited.

When she didn't believe, He didn't leave.

She has tried to love others the way He loved her—not perfectly, but stubbornly.

And sometimes, when she looks at the crucifix, she whispers, "You're the only one who never turned away."

He is still the only man who never demanded of her to be less.

Echo—Inspired by Love That Shaped, Scarred, and Stirred the Soul

They didn't rescue me.
But they saw me—
each in their own fractured way.
One opened the world.
One broke the cage.
One tried to build a smaller one
and call it safety.
They all loved me.
Even when they didn't understand how.
Even when I didn't know how to be loved.
They left fingerprints,
not chains.
And I carry them still—
not as burdens,
but as echoes
of who I was,
and who I could no longer be.

18

The Women Who Carried Me

Some Carried Me in Prayer. Some in Protest. All in Love

Not all saints wear halos.
    Some wear aprons, headscarves, lipstick, or worn-out boots.
    Some teach with theology. Others with soup.
    These are the women who carried Hope—through wilderness, through wonder, through war.

Mama

She carried Hope in her womb, then in her silence.
    A strong woman. Not soft. But steady.
    She didn't say "I love you" often. But she stayed. Through blackouts, shortages, secrets. Through the morning Hope confessed her fear that God had forgotten her.
    Her mother only said, "Then I will remember you for Him."
    They still speak by phone when the war allows.
    Each call ends the same.
    "Be good, Hope."
    "I'm trying, Mama."

Babushka Elena

The village mystic. Half-blind, half-legend. Entirely holy.

She prayed the rosary with hands that had buried sons.

She once looked Hope in the eye and said, "Child, don't fear the fire. You were made from it."

Hope didn't understand then.

She does now.

The Girl with the Boat

Yes—a real boat.

She was a licensed yacht captain, a ski instructor, and the kind of woman who could steer through storms and laugh while doing it. Fearless, radiant, unforgettable.

She was Hope's dear friend. They met during a season when everything felt adrift—and this woman, wild and free, was an anchor in the most unexpected way.

She once fell deeply in love—so much so that the thought of giving it up for religious life almost broke her.

Still, she tried.

She entered the convent. Lasted three weeks.

Not because she was weak, but because that kind of decision demands you amputate something sacred—and in her case, it was a love she couldn't cut off without bleeding.

When she left, the grief came hard.

Not just for the relationship, but for the realization that her sense of self had been wrapped tightly around someone else.

She spiraled into a quiet depression—a deep ache masked by her usual fire. Hope saw it. Sat with it. Knew what it meant to rebuild from that kind of hollow.

She loved her fiercely. Still does.

Because this woman taught Hope that strength isn't just about surviving the sea.

Sometimes, it's about knowing when to come back to shore.

Three Sisters

Not religious. Just real.

Three women—bold, warm, fiercely loyal—who opened their home like it was normal to invite grace in for dinner.

They made Hope part of their family without a ceremony.

She had Christmas with them.

Laughter in their kitchen.

Blankets and secrets and second helpings.

They never asked her to explain where she had been or what she had left behind.

They just said, "Stay."

They loved her the way women do when they're not threatened by each other's strength—but made stronger by it.

Hope never forgot them.

The ones who offered tissues, tea, truth.

The ones who braided her hair, held her doubts, reminded her who she was.

Not one of them was perfect.

But every single one was a mirror of mercy.

Renia

A fellow sister. Wild with questions. Once wrote feminist theology on napkins during lunch breaks.

Renia wasn't safe—but she was true.

She told Hope, "Don't confuse obedience with absence of self."

They argued often. Prayed louder. Laughed harder.

When Renia left the convent, Hope grieved like a breakup.

They still exchange emails full of poems and unsent letters to God.

Sister Judy

Her local superior. Gruff. Blunt. Brilliant.

Taught her how to iron a habit and how to defend a doctrine.

Also taught her that tears aren't weakness—they're saltwater cleaning wounds.

When Hope wanted to quit formation, Judy simply handed her a crucifix and said, "Hold on when you don't believe. That's when He does."

She died before Hope took final vows.

Hope still carries her rosary.

Aurelia

An old woman in a soup line in Slovakia.

She gave Hope a wool scarf in winter, even though she had only one.

When Hope refused, Aurelia said, "Child, take it. Or I'll be offended. It's rude to reject love."

Marla

The one who asked the question.

The one who made room.

The one who didn't flinch.

Marla wasn't a nun. Wasn't pious. She drank strong coffee and cursed when politics came up.

But she listened like a confessor and loved like a mother.

Hope still believes Marla saved her life—not with theology, but with space.

The Girl in the Mirror

Hope saw her one morning after a retreat. Tired eyes. Hair uneven. Cheeks softer than she remembered.

She didn't look holy.

But she looked *alive*.

The Women Who Carried Me

And for the first time in years, Hope whispered to the girl in the mirror, "I'm glad you're still here."

They carried her.
In silence. In laughter. In memory. In wine and ashes and bread.
She carries them now—every time she comforts, teaches, stays.
Because that's what women do.
We carry each other until we can stand again.

Echo—Inspired by Women Who Held, Healed, and Stayed

They didn't need to fix me.
They just stayed.
With blankets.
With bread.
With stories that said
"You're not alone."
Some held my hand
while I fell apart.
Some passed the tea
and never asked why my eyes were red.
They taught me that strength
is not the absence of breaking—
but the grace of still being here,
together.
I never had sisters.
But I have been sistered.
And I will never forget
the women who carried me home.

19

Letting Go

The Lioness

Some Call It Leaving. She Calls It Resurrection

Letting go didn't come all at once.

It came in pieces. Like petals falling from a flower that had bloomed long past its season.

At first, Hope ignored the signs.

The fatigue she couldn't pray away.

The ache she couldn't name.

The moments when silence no longer felt like communion, but confinement.

She kept smiling. Kept serving. Kept believing that if she just tried harder, it would all feel holy again.

But grace had shifted.

What once felt like vocation now felt like weight.

The veil itched. The schedule felt suffocating.

She used to wake up with joy. Now she woke up with dread.

One night, after a parish council meeting that left her feeling invisible, she walked to the chapel and sat in the dark.

She didn't light a candle.

She just sat.

Letting Go

And said the words she had been afraid to say for months:
"I think... I'm done."
The silence that followed didn't feel like judgment.
It felt like permission.

She tried to talk herself out of it.
Made lists. Pros. Cons. Scriptures. Fears.
She consulted superiors. Some were kind. Others were disappointed.
One asked, "Are you sure this isn't just a spiritual dryness?"
Hope looked them in the eye and said, "This isn't dryness. This is clarity."

She grieved, of course.
Grieved the dreams she had dressed in linen.
Grieved the girl who thought vows would fix the ache.
Grieved the Sisters who had become family, the rhythms of prayer, the little things—like lighting candles before dawn, or ironing altar cloths while humming hymns.
But underneath the grief... was peace.
And a strange kind of lightness.
As if a chapter had closed, not in shame—but in completion.

On the day she left, she folded her habit carefully.
Not like something discarded.
But like something sacred that had done its work.
She whispered "Thank you" as she packed.
To whom?
She wasn't sure.
Maybe God.
Maybe herself.
Maybe the girl who first said yes without knowing how much it would cost—or how much it would heal.

Letting go didn't mean failure.
It meant honoring the truth.

And sometimes, the holiest thing you can do . . . is walk away before you forget how to walk at all.

Echo—Inspired by the Letting Go That Made Room for Becoming

I thought letting go
would feel like weakness.
But it felt like truth.
And truth is never soft.
I grieved what I could not fix.
I blessed what I had to leave.
And then I stood up
Lighter
but not less.
Not healed,
but whole in the way only those
who have lost everything
can be.
I did not roar.
I did not run.
I simply stayed standing.
That was enough.

20

After

**Not an Ending. Not Quite a Beginning.
Only the Slow Relearning of Breath**

Life after the convent wasn't glamorous.

There were no fireworks. No sudden clarity. Just rent payments, awkward introductions, and learning how to wear jeans again without feeling exposed.

Hope moved into a tiny apartment with mismatched furniture and a kettle that whistled like an old woman gossiping.

She didn't rush to "find her purpose."

She had chased purpose for years.

Now, she just wanted to *live*.

Some days were easy.

She made omelets. Watered plants. Woke up to sunlight instead of a bell. Prayed when she felt like it. Cried when she needed to.

Other days were messier.

She missed the rhythm. The certainty. The reverence of a chapel at midnight.

But she didn't miss the smallness she had begun to feel.

Now, there was space—in her schedule, in her soul.

Broken Things Sing Too

She started writing again.

Not to impress. Not to preach.

Just to remember.

She wrote down stories. Not all of them hers.

Stories about lost boys and tired women. About God showing up in wrong places, wearing strange disguises.

She sent one to a small publication.

They wrote back.

"We'd like to publish this. Do you have more?"

Hope stared at the email for a long time.

Then smiled.

She made new friends—messy ones, bold ones, skeptical ones. People who loved God in fragments and didn't always get the words right.

They called her Hope.

Just Hope.

No titles. No "Sister."

And slowly, she grew into her name.

One morning, walking through a park in late spring, she heard a busker singing a tune that tugged at something old in her chest.

The lyrics were new.

But the ache was familiar.

"Broken things sing too," the man sang.

She stopped.

Listened.

Let the tears come without hiding.

She wasn't healed.

But she was whole.

And that, she had learned, was more than enough.

After

Echo—Not Healed. Not Undone. Just Breathing Without Flinching

I woke up
and the air was mine.
No rules.
No locked doors.
Just sunlight on the floor
and a passport with pages to fill.
I bought flowers for no reason.
Took trains with no destination.
Slept diagonally
in a bed too big for guilt.
I was a bird out of the cage,
a butterfly without a map—
fluttering from wonder to wonder,
refusing to land too soon.
It wasn't about finding one place.
It was about tasting life
in every color
before choosing where to stay.

21

When You Don't Belong Anywhere

Between Countries, Between Callings, Between Names

Even after letting go, Hope thought freedom would feel cleaner.

Instead, it felt like standing barefoot on gravel—unsure which direction hurts less.

She had left the convent.

She had stayed in the Church.

But she no longer knew where she fit.

Too strange for the secular world.

Too scarred for religious life.

Too intense for small talk.

Too soft for bureaucracy.

She volunteered. Consulted. Wrote grant proposals. Led workshops.

But inside, she was drifting.

She tried one job in parish ministry.

The people were kind. The walls were beige.

The meetings were eternal.

She felt invisible again—but this time without a habit to explain the absence.

A priest once asked her, "Are you planning to get married now?"

She blinked. "I'm planning to breathe."

She lived in three places that year.
> Each time she unpacked, she whispered, "Maybe this is it."
> Each time she repacked, she whispered, "Maybe it wasn't."

But then something changed.
> Not in the world—in her.
> She stopped waiting for arrival.
> And started honoring movement.
> She was still Hope.
> Even if Hope didn't come with a job title or a defined role.
> And somehow, that was enough.
> For now.

Echo—Inspired by the Ache of Not Belonging— and the Quiet Hope of Becoming

I walked into rooms
where no one spoke my language—
and into others
where they spoke it
but still didn't see me.
I smiled politely.
Translated my soul.
Tried on customs
like borrowed coats.
I belonged everywhere
and nowhere.
But slowly,
I stopped searching for the perfect fit.
And started listening

Broken Things Sing Too

to the sound of my own footsteps
on strange, beautiful roads.
Maybe home isn't a place.
Maybe it's the path
you walk
when no one else is watching.

22

Invisible Work

The Kind of Work That Doesn't Go on Resumes—but Builds the Soul

Hope worked behind the scenes again.
　She helped translate church documents. Coached catechists. Planned retreats for people who forgot to say thank you.
　She was never in the bulletin.
　But she was in the sacristy at 6:00 a.m., fixing torn altar cloths before anyone noticed.
　She was the one people called when someone died suddenly.
　The one who knew which teenager was about to crack.
　The one who stayed late to fold chairs after every speaker left the stage.

Sometimes, she resented it.
　The way others took credit.
　The way bishops praised the loud ones.
　The way parish councils smiled at her and called her "support staff."
　But most days, she remembered:
　Christ wasn't on the stage.

He was in the back—breaking bread, washing feet.
And so was she.

She didn't need applause.
But sometimes, she needed someone to say, "I see what you're doing. And it matters."
God said it once—not in words, but in the way a crying child clung to her shoulder after a parent left.
That was enough.

Echo—Inspired by the Sacred Labor No One Sees

It didn't make headlines.
No photos, no speeches,
just lights turned off,
children fed,
wounds cleaned
that no one knew were there.
I led from behind.
I carried what others dropped.
I made peace
and tea
and miracles no one named.
Some days I wanted to scream:
"See me."
But most days,
I just kept going.
This is the holy work—
not always loud,
but always faithful.
The kind that builds kingdoms
without ever needing
a throne.

23

Why I Still Believe

It's Not Because Life Got Easier.
It's Because Love Got Louder

People often asked her, after all the loss and unraveling, "Do you still believe?"

Hope never answered quickly.

Because belief wasn't something she could measure anymore.

Not in rosaries, not in Mass attendance, not even in her ability to pray out loud.

But yes.

She still believed.

Not because she'd seen miracles.

But because she'd seen mercy.

She believed in the Christ who wept.

In the Spirit who groaned.

In the Father who waited at the gate longer than anyone thought reasonable.

She didn't always believe in the system.

Or the rules.

Or the men with collars who forgot how to kneel.

But she still believed in Jesus.
Because when everyone else left, He didn't.

She had walked away from many things.
But every time she tried to walk away from Him, He showed up:
In the child who asked for a hug.
In the stranger who paid her bus fare.
In the wind on a morning she wanted to disappear.

Hope didn't believe out of certainty anymore.
She believed out of memory. Out of ache. Out of some stubborn flame that refused to go out.
She believed because she had seen too much beauty to give up.
And because even in the silence,
God had never stopped whispering, "I'm still here."

Echo—I Still Kneel

I do not kneel because I have no questions.
I kneel because my questions won't let me stand.
I do not pray because I feel holy.
I pray because I forget how to breathe.
I do not sing because the song is easy.
I sing because silence was killing me.
I do not believe because the Church convinced me.
I believe because Love kept showing up when I stopped looking.
I still kneel.
Not always in pews.
Sometimes on bathroom floors.
Sometimes in traffic.
Sometimes in the messy middle of a Monday.
But I still kneel.
Because somewhere beneath the ache,
I still trust the hands that made me.

Why I Still Believe

Echo—Inspired by Faith That Stayed, Even When Everything Else Left

I lost the answers.
But I never stopped whispering
into the dark.
Not because I was sure—
but because something in me remembered
how it felt
to be held.
He didn't always speak.
But I still lit the candle.
Still broke the bread.
Still waited
with my face turned toward the silence
like it was morning.
I don't believe because it's easy
I believe because
even in the breaking,
I was never alone.

24

The Church That Hurt Me

And the Christ Who Stayed Anyway

Hope had loved the Church since she found God.
    Loved the incense. The ancient chants. The mystery of a God who made Himself bread.
    She gave her whole life to it.
    And for a long time, that love felt enough.

But then came the moments no one prepares you for.
    The priest who made comments he shouldn't have.
    The bishop who spoke of mercy but lived for control.
    The women who smiled at her and cut her down behind closed doors.
    The abuse. The cover-ups. The public apologies followed by private arrogance.
    The meetings where trauma was treated as inconvenience.
    The decisions made by men who never asked what it felt like to bleed in the pews.

The Church That Hurt Me

She stopped praying in groups for a while.

Not because she lost faith—but because she couldn't bear the way prayer had been used to manipulate, to silence, to shame.

She prayed in stairwells instead.

In whispered "help me" prayers between hospital visits.

In choked thank-yous at stoplights.

And in long, wordless sobs in the chapel after another survivor told her story.

One night, while journaling in frustration, she wrote:

"I love the Church. But it doesn't always love me back."

She didn't mean to write it.

But it was true.

And still.

Still . . .

She stayed.

Not for the hierarchy.

Not for the buildings.

But for the broken.

The weeping.

The searching.

The quiet ones who lit candles with trembling hands.

And because Jesus had never told her to leave.

Only to stay awake.

Hope didn't leave the Church.

She left the room where her soul was suffocating.

One night, after weeks of sleepless wrestling, Hope finally told her spiritual director she was leaving the congregation.

He didn't shout. He didn't plead.

He just asked, quietly—

"When you close your eyes for the last time . . . how will you be able to look into Jesus' eyes?"

She didn't flinch.

She simply answered,

"How will *He* be able to look into *my* eyes when we meet?"
It wasn't rebellion.
It was a heart breaking open—not away from Christ, but toward the Christ she had always known:
The One who weeps.
The One who stays.
The One who never asked her to disappear to be holy.
She wasn't turning from Him.
She was turning toward the only version of Him she could still trust.

Echo—Inspired by a Love That Won't Pretend

I stayed long after it hurt
because I thought He asked me to.
I called it obedience.
He called it silence.
But when the voices of men
grew louder than the voice of God,
I stopped listening to them.
If He is love,
He will not flinch when I ask
what love would never have done.
When I meet Him,
He will see my eyes,
and they will still be open.

25

Grief Comes in Seasons

It Doesn't Ask Permission. It Just
Arrives, Again and Again

Grief wasn't a one-time visitor.
>It came in waves.
>Sometimes tidal. Sometimes quiet.
>Always unexpected.
>Hope had buried many things.
>A country she couldn't return to.
>A vocation she once called home.
>People she loved.
>Versions of herself she would never see again.
>And each grief had its own season.

Some seasons were loud.
>Like the first Lent after she left the convent—when ashes felt too honest and resurrection too far away.
>Or the week her friend died of cancer, and Hope had to lead a retreat the next day, smiling through a liturgy she could barely say.

Some seasons were slow.
> Like the months after the war began.
> The ache of checking messages every morning, holding her breath until her family answered.
> Or the quiet grief of watching others live the life she once imagined—weddings, baptisms, traditions she never got to build.

People expected healing to be linear.
> But Hope knew better.
> Healing looped back on itself.
> It circled. It revisited.
> It came in grocery store music, in old photos, in unexpected kindness that made the ache feel real again.

One autumn morning, while raking leaves outside a retreat center, she cried without knowing why.
> Then realized:
> "Grief is remembering that love once had a home in me. And now it lives in memory."

She didn't fight it anymore.
> Grief, she had learned, was not her enemy.
> It was a sign she still had a heart.
> And that heart, though broken, still beat.

Echo—Inspired by Grief That Doesn't Leave, but Learns to Breathe with You

It doesn't follow the calendar.
It arrives in the scent of rain,
a song in a café,
the way someone laughs
just like they did.
It softens—
but it never fully leaves.
Some days I carry it

Grief Comes in Seasons

like a child asleep on my chest.
Other days,
like a storm I can't see through.
But always,
grief is proof
that something mattered.
And if I must carry it,
I will carry it like a candle—
Lit
and trembling,
but never hidden.

26

God of the In-Between

The God Who Stays, Even When Nothing Else Makes Sense

Hope used to think God lived in the peaks.

The mountaintop moments.

The clean conversions.

The joy-soaked retreats and candlelit hymns.

And yes, God was there.

But later, in the years after loss and war and vocational unraveling, she found Him somewhere stranger:

In the waiting rooms.

In the long drives home.

In the mornings when she didn't want to get out of bed.

She began to call Him the God of the In-Between.

Not the God of arrival.

Not the God of clarity.

But the God who sat beside her in the fog and didn't rush her forward.

God of the In-Between

She met Him on long walks without answers.
    In piles of laundry that no one thanked her for.
    In the stare of a woman at the back of a church who whispered, "Pray for my son. He's using again."
    Hope didn't have words.
    So she offered her presence.
    And somehow, that was enough.

One night, during Adoration, she prayed, "Lord, I don't know where I'm going anymore."
    And in the silence, she sensed:
    "You don't need to know. You just need to stay close."

The in-between no longer felt like failure.
    It felt like invitation.
    To trust.
    To breathe.
    To keep walking, even when the map had been taken away.
    Because the God of the In-Between?
    He was never lost.

Echo—Inspired by the Space Between Dying and Deciding to Live

It wasn't one bad convent.
It wasn't one cruel sister.
It was twenty years
of dying in pieces
with a smile on my face
and obedience in my mouth.
Gaslit in the name of God.
Silence used like a whip.
Sacrifice demanded
until I had nothing left to bleed.
I wanted to die.
Not because I lost faith—

Broken Things Sing Too

but because I couldn't find Him
in their voices anymore.
But somehow,
in the in-between,
He whispered.
Not loud.
Not commanding.
Just present.
And that was enough
to keep breathing.
Not for them.
Not even for me.
But for the God
who stayed behind
when everyone else used His name
to disappear.

27

What I've Learned About Healing

It's Rarely What We Expect. And Never What We Can Rush.

Hope used to think healing would look like triumph.

Like scars fading. Like certainty returning. Like walking forward without flinching.

But healing, as it turned out, was quieter.

Messier.

And surprisingly ordinary.

She learned that healing wasn't a before-and-after story.

It was a mosaic—broken pieces rearranged into something beautiful but different than the original design.

She learned:

- Sometimes healing looks like getting out of bed and brushing your teeth.
- Sometimes it's saying "no" without apology.
- Sometimes it's not crying when you talk about it—and sometimes it's finally letting yourself cry.

She learned that healing isn't linear.
> That grief revisits.
> That old wounds speak in new seasons.
> That someone's tone of voice can reopen something you thought was buried.
> But she also learned that love goes deeper than pain.
> That laughter still bubbles up.
> That joy can be rebellious.

One of the biggest surprises was this:
> You don't have to be fully healed to be holy.
> You don't have to be whole to be helpful.
> You don't have to be fixed to be faithful.

She still had hard days.
> But she stopped shaming herself for them.
> Because healing, she realized, wasn't about becoming perfect.
> It was about becoming real.
> And that . . . was sacred.

Echo—Inspired by the Joy of Healing, and the Song Only Broken Things Can Sing

Healing didn't look like I expected.
Not neat.
Not linear.
Not clean.
It looked like music too loud in the kitchen.
Like dancing barefoot while the soup boils over.
Like laughing with my head back—
and not apologizing.
It looked like crying in public
and not caring who watched.
It looked like saying yes
to dresses,
and mountains,

What I've Learned About Healing

and late-night flights
just because I can.
I am not untouched.
But I am alive.
And somehow,
the cracks have become
the very place
where the music gets in.
Broken things sing too.

28

Home Isn't a Place

It's What Stays When Everything Else Moves

Hope used to think *home* was a building.
    Maybe the convent. Maybe her family's apartment in Ukraine. Maybe a chapel that smelled like incense and wood polish.
    But then she lost all of those.
    And still—something in her remained grounded.
    That's when she started to learn:
    Home isn't where you are.
    Home is what holds you when you don't know where you are.

Sometimes, home was a friend who texted, "Just checking on you."
    Sometimes, it was the ritual of holding a morning coffee with too much milk and no rush.
    Sometimes, it was a familiar psalm in an unfamiliar city.

She lived in many places after leaving religious life.
    Guest rooms. Studios. Church basements.
    Each time she unpacked, she placed her candle and journal on the nightstand like a quiet declaration:
    I'm here now. This is enough.

She missed belonging—not just to a place, but to people who *got* her.

But slowly, gently, she began to realize:
She belonged to God.
She belonged to the ache that shaped her.
She belonged to the stories she now had the courage to tell.

One afternoon, after speaking at a retreat, a woman hugged her and whispered, "Thank you. I felt at home in your story."

Hope smiled.

Because maybe *that* was the point all along.

To carry home within her—and offer it to others.

Echo—Inspired by the Journey from Rootlessness to Rootedness

I spent years searching for a door
that would open with my name on it.
A room where I didn't have to explain
my voice,
my past,
my joy.
But no place held all of me.
Not country,
not convent,
not childhood street.
So I stopped searching
and started planting.
Books on the shelf.
Tea in the cupboard.
Friends who know which silence means "stay."
And on the door—
a sign that says:
"Welcome-ish. Depending who you are
and how long you stay."
Because I've learned

Broken Things Sing Too

that peace deserves protection.
And love is still welcome.
But now,
so am I.
Home isn't a place.
It's a choice.
And I've made mine.

29

Things I Didn't Say

Not Because I Couldn't. Because I Wasn't Ready

Some stories Hope kept in silence.
    Not out of shame—but because she was still learning their language.
    Not everything she lived fit neatly into testimony.
    Not every ache had a resolution.
    Some truths were too fragile to share in front of microphones.
    So here are a few of the things she didn't say . . .

She didn't say how lonely religious life could be.
    That you can live in community and still feel unknown.
    That sometimes, it's easier to serve than to be seen.

She didn't say how hard it was to leave.
    That even when it's the right choice, it still feels like betrayal.
    That you can grieve the loss of a life you no longer want.

She didn't say how many nights she stared at the ceiling, wondering:
    Did I disappoint God?
    Did I imagine my calling?

Will I ever feel that close to heaven again?

She didn't say how many times she almost fell in love after.
> How many times she didn't.
> How often she wondered if healing meant being alone forever.

She didn't say how her body still flinched when people raised their voices.
> Or how she kept a packed bag in her closet for years—just in case she had to run again.

But maybe silence is holy too.
> Not every story has to be told to be real.
> And maybe the most sacred things . . . are the ones God hears first.

Echo—Inspired by the Weight of Words Left Unspoken

There were things
I never said out loud.
Not because I didn't feel them,
but because there wasn't space,
or safety,
or anyone who knew how to listen.
I didn't say:
"I'm scared."
"I'm angry."
"That broke me."
"Please stay."
I carried them in my spine,
in the tension behind my smile,
in the poems I never wrote.
But silence is not forgetfulness.
And now,
every breath I take

Things I Didn't Say

makes room
for what was buried.
I may not say it all.
But I am no longer silent.

30

What Hope Knows Now

Not Everything. But Enough

Hope doesn't have all the answers.

She's made peace with that.

She no longer believes healing is a destination or that vocation comes with a permanent address.

But she knows a few things now—things that took tears, silence, and surrender to learn.

She knows:

- You can love something deeply and still let it go.
- God is bigger than the roles we play for Him.
- Some prayers are just breathing—and that's enough.

She knows grace sometimes comes disguised as failure.

That the people who break your heart can also be the ones who teach you how to rebuild it.

She knows that even after war, betrayal, leaving, grief—you can still laugh.

Loudly.

And mean it.

Hope knows she is not what she lost.
> She is what she became after.
> She knows faith isn't certainty—it's choosing to stay open when you have every reason to close.

And she knows that broken things—like hearts, like stories, like hymns in the dark—can still sing.

Final Benediction—Becoming Me

They taught me
that being a woman
was a weakness.
A wound.
A thing to hide
or to tame.
They made silence
my second skin.
Shame
my shadow.
But I am done apologizing
for softness that holds storms.
For tears that speak truth.
For a body,
a voice,
a soul
that belongs only to me.
I am not less
because I feel deeply.
I am not wrong
because I rise differently.
I am a woman.
I am all of me.
And I will never
shrink again.

Epilogue
A Letter from Hope

Dear reader,

    If you made it here, thank you.

    For walking with me through shadow and silence.

    Through loss and light.

    Through stories that were sometimes mine . . . and maybe, sometimes, yours too.

    I didn't write this because I had everything figured out.

    I wrote it because I didn't.

    Because I needed to name the ache—and remember that even the jagged pieces can catch the light.

If you've ever left something sacred,
    or stayed longer than you should have,
    or asked God a question He hasn't answered yet—
You are not alone.
    If you've ever carried grief quietly,
    or laughed at the wrong time,
    or loved someone who couldn't stay—
You are not strange.
You are brave.

I still believe.
    Not in perfection.
    But in the quiet resilience of the human spirit.

Broken Things Sing Too

In the kindness of strangers.
In the echo of God in the most unlikely places.

So if you are still healing . . .
    still hoping . . .
    still learning how to breathe again—
    Come sit beside me.
    There's room.
    And remember:
    Broken things sing too.

With you,
    Hope

www.ingramcontent.com/pod-product-compliance
Lightning Source LLC
Chambersburg PA
CBHW071714040426
42446CB00011B/2064